Five Little Dinosaurs

Written by Fay Robinson • Illustrated by Claude Martinot

2   Five little dinosaurs are running out the door.

One stops to make a snack.
And then there are four.

3

4   Four little dinosaurs are hiding under trees.

One stops to take a nap.
And then there are three.

5

6   Three little dinosaurs are going to the zoo.

One stops to take a swim.
And then there are two.

8   Two little dinosaurs are playing in the sun.

One stops to read this book.
And then there is one.

One little dinosaur is playing in the park.

He stops when he is done.
And then it's almost dark!

11

Five little dinosaurs are sitting all alone.

All hear a great big ROARRRR!!!

And then they head for home!